My Fat Saiᴅ

A Devotional

TRILOGY

My Father Said
Trilogy Christian Publishers A Wholly Owned Subsidiary of
Trinity Broadcasting Network
2442 Michelle Drive Tustin, CA 92780
Copyright © 2022 by H. S. Morgan

Rights Department, 2442 Michelle Drive, Tustin, CA 92780.

Trilogy Christian Publishing/TBN and colophon are trademarks
of Trinity Broadcasting Network.

Cover design by: Natalee Groves

For information about special discounts for bulk purchases,
please contact Trilogy Christian Publishing.

Trilogy Disclaimer: The views and content expressed in this
book are those of the author and may not necessarily reflect
the views and doctrine of Trilogy Christian Publishing or the
Trinity Broadcasting Network.

Manufactured in the United States of America

10 9 8 7 6 5 4 3 2 1

Library of Congress Cataloging-in-Publication Data is
available.

ISBN: 978-1-63769-810-5
E-ISBN: 978-1-63769-811-2

The author, His Servant, has chosen to give God ALL the glory by maintaining its anonymity. His Servant is also regarded as "HS," the Holy Spirit, Who inspired these readings.

DEDICATION

In dedication to my Heavenly Father and
to my natural father.

Acknowledgment

It is my heart's desire that I will *never* lose my place in You, Lord. It is indeed such a sweet place. I have found a *resting place*, and that place is in You. I don't have to look any farther because I have found a friend and a lover in You. *You are my best friend and lover! Nobody* can be to me as You are, Lord. No, not one! I love You, I love You, and I love You so much, so very much, Lord, all the way from the crown of my head to my lower extremities, to the tips of my toes, and down to the soles of my feet. I am filled to overflowing with Your love. Nothing else could ever satisfy, and neither can anyone else.

Your love is matchless! It's fulfilling and overpowering. It has and is lifting me to heights that I have never known. I could just fly away to heaven and live forever in Your Presence where there is no limit to express my love for You. I look forward to the day that You will come to take me home.

While there is still time, I hope and pray to leave my physical house in order. It is my goal to owe no man anything but love. I am purposing to be about building Your Kingdom. It is one of my biggest desires to win many, many souls for You. Also, I intend to complete every assignment You have given me in excellence. I shall make it my aim to reach my fullest potential of serving You and living for You on this side of heaven.

Here's looking forward to that great day when I shall see You face to face. Then I will be ready to place my crowns at Your feet. I shall praise You, worship You, honor You, and love You forever and ever throughout everlasting life. I hope and pray that it will be so! In Your Precious, Wonderful, Majestic, Matchless, Righteous, and Holy Name, Jesus!

—His Servant

TABLE OF CONTENTS

Foreword

My natural father said, "It is okay if you have made a mistake if you have an eraser. Learn from your mistake and try not to make that mistake again." It has been revealed to me that the eraser is the forgiveness of the Lord, Jesus Christ.

I have learned that along my journey, I would fall prey to making many mistakes. I have learned from those mistakes, and I have not purposely repeated them. However, I have also learned that a lesson unlearned shall be repeated.

My Heavenly Father said a lot of things. He has given us sixty-six books as evidence of His wisdom. I have found a wealth of wisdom, direction, love, joy, peace, and comfort within the pages of God's Holy Bible. I have found a resting place in Him. My soul is content, and my anchor of hope rests in Him alone.

It would behoove each reader to listen for God's voice and for His wisdom as He speaks in these conversations with me.

INTRODUCTION

This book is to inspire the reader by reading conversations between the Heavenly Father, via the Holy Spirit, and one of His children. It's like reading someone's mail. Hopefully, you will be able to identify with what God is saying as if He were speaking directly to you. You are given lines to express "Your Thoughts or Prayers" to God in response to what you interpret. The aim is for you to develop a fine-tune, listening ear for hearing God's voice. Therefore, you should be able to:

1. Focus on what is being said
2. Determine whether you can relate to what is said or how it relates to you
3. Develop the discipline of daily writing
4. Decide how you will apply what was said into your daily life
5. Decipher whether the daily readings provoke you to affirmation or to conviction
6. Resist the denial of the need to change
7. Try to draw closer to God
8. Prepare for the Lord's soon return.

Day One

Keep your heart open to Me, God. If your heart is open, your ears shall be open, and if your ears are open, your eyes shall be opened. Then, you shall indeed hear Me and see Me. If you close your heart to Me, you will not be able to hear Me, and if you are not able to hear Me, you will not be able to see Me. Therefore, you will not be able to walk with Me. Do you recognize that the word "ear" is inside of "heart"? That is why your heart must be purified. It opens your ears and your eyes to be able to hear Me and to see Me.

Can you follow My lead or My instructions if you can't hear Me? Can you follow My leading if you cannot see Me? Your ears and your eyes are connected to your heart. I live inside of your heart by way of your ears and your eyes. The Holy Spirit speaks from out of My heart to your ears because He dwells in your heart. You have heard that the issues of your life flow out of your heart. Listen often for My voice so that you may hear Me in order to see Me and to follow Me as I lead the way.

Your Thoughts or Prayer

_____

_____

_____

_____

_____

_____

_____

_____

_____

_____

_____

_____

_____

_____

_____

_____

_____

_____

_____

_____

_____

_____

Day Two

I have thoroughly enjoyed the time spent with you during this morning's fellowship. I enjoyed every one of the songs you sang to Me. Thank you for singing them from your heart and making melody to the throne of My heart. Your love for Me is so very evident. Oh, how I wish all My people would love Me and express their love to Me as you do! The more I would express My Love to them.

Thank you, My child, for receiving My Love. As you know, to receive My Love is to receive Me because, as it has been revealed to you, I Am love. To receive more of My love is to receive more of Me. For many, to say and to hear "God loves you" is just a warm and fuzzy scripture. To get or to receive the fullest revelation of "God loves you" is to understand that I, God, "Gods you." That means that I fill you up with Me/My love. You will become so full of Me that you can't help but be a big light in this dark dying world. The Light of Me will dispel the darkness and draw all to Me. It's an invisible work but real work. So, be the light, My child. Shine bright for Me!

Your Thoughts or Prayer

_____

_____

_____

_____

_____

_____

_____

_____

_____

_____

_____

_____

_____

_____

_____

_____

_____

_____

_____

_____

_____

DAY THREE

You coming to spend time with Me is a blessing to Me. To hear you say that you desire to start and end your day with Me is so very special. Yes, I love for you to sing praises and make melody to Me. I receive your love and adoration for Me. Being loved by Me and reciprocating My Love is a two-way street. True love is and does just that. Thank you for receiving My Love for you, My dear, and thank you for loving Me back. It's called the circle of love, and it's a never-ending love from the Father to His child. In your case, it's the love of the Father to His child and the love of a child to its Father. No one shares this circle but you and I. Our circle of love connects to others, and for each person you love, it's a one-on-one circle of love with that individual. In other words, see each relationship that you have with each person as another circle of love. Nurture each circle as often as you can. You will be spreading the love of Me, your Heavenly Father, with each. You should now see that I am Love, and Love is God. You, therefore, are building circles of love with Me and for Me. Thank you, My child, for loving Me and for sharing Me and My love with others.

Your Thoughts or Prayer

_____

_____

_____

_____

_____

_____

_____

_____

_____

_____

_____

_____

_____

_____

_____

_____

_____

_____

_____

Day Four

Thank you so very much for singing to Me this morning. You sang "I Sing Praises to Your Name." You really blessed Me. Thank you for recognizing Who I Am by My Name. You sang "My Name Is King Jesus," which means I Am Sovereign and that I rule. You sang "Hallelujah to My Name," which means all praises to My Name. You sang "How Excellent Is My Name," which means there is no lack or flaw in My Name. You also sang "My Name is Great and Greatly to Be Praised," "There Is No Other Name Like My Name," and "My Name Is Jesus."

You apologized to Me for your wandering mind as you sang to Me. The enemy will attempt to distract you from keeping your mind focused on Me. But because of My Sovereignty, he has fought a losing battle. You recognized that you drifted in your mind as your heart and mouth continued to sing to Me. It is in your heart, My child, that I live. It is in Me that you live, move, and have your being. Even though your mind was distracted by the enemy, your heart was protected by Me. It's your heart that I seek, not your performance. Your heart belongs to Me. Thank you for giving your heart to Me and for singing praises to Me.

Your Thoughts or Prayer

_____

_____

_____

_____

_____

_____

_____

_____

_____

_____

_____

_____

_____

_____

_____

_____

_____

_____

DAY FIVE

It blesses Me how you have delighted yourself in Me this morning. You spent the whole one-on-one time describing Me by each letter of the alphabet. You said or rather you sang "How Excellent Is Your Name." You sang that My Name is:

1—Abba	10—Joy	19—Savior
2—Beautiful	11—Kind	20—Truth
3—Christ	12—Love	21—Understanding
4—Daddy	13—Merciful	22—Victorious
5—Excellent	14—Nurturer	23—Wonderful
6—Faithful	15—Omnipotent	24—Xtraordinary
7—Great	16—Peace	25—Yahweh
8—Hope	17—Quiet	26—Zoe
9—Infinite	18—Rest	27—And More

As you know and spoke to Me afterward, My Name is inexhaustible, or inexhaustive! There is no limit to Who I Am called, Who I can be, nor What I can do. Thank you, My child, for delighting yourself in Who I Am with your precious name-calling. Continue to focus on Who I Am, as I purpose to manifest more of Who I Am in you so that you shall look, sound, think, and be more like your Daddy God. Remember, in you I live, I move, and I have My Being. In you, I Am. Delight yourself in Me, and I will give you the right desires of your heart.

Your Thoughts or Prayer

_____

_____

_____

_____

_____

_____

_____

_____

_____

_____

_____

_____

_____

_____

_____

_____

_____

_____

DAY SIX

I have enjoyed the praises that you sang to Me this morning. I shall call you My morning songbird. Thank you, My child, for choosing to talk to Me first before talking to others and for ignoring your text calls like the one you received this morning. You demonstrated to Me that nothing or no one is more important to you than the time you spend with Me. You are not letting anything interrupt Our time together. Know that Our time is so very precious to Me. It makes Me feel that I Am special to you. Yes, I do know all things, My dear, but I also like to feel good. So, hearing your songs of praises was indeed good music to My ears and to My heart. Seeing you choose not to look at your unidentified text message made Me feel good and special. Thank you, again, for making Me feel special, My child. You started with singing, "Way-maker, miracle-worker, promise-keeper/and light in the darkness." Yes, that is Who I Am and shall always be, My child, to you and to others. It is true and more than just a nice-sounding song. Expect Me to manifest Myself as each one in your life. I, the promise-keeper, shall always keep My Promises.

Your Thoughts or Prayer

_____

_____

_____

_____

_____

_____

_____

_____

_____

_____

_____

_____

_____

_____

_____

_____

_____

_____

_____

DAY SEVEN

Once again, you sang praises to My Name. Oh, how I enjoy your singing. This morning you sang:

"How Excellent Is My Name"

"King Jesus Is My Name"

"Glory to My Name

"How Majestic Is My Name"

Oh, how I wish that the whole wide world would know Me by My Names. I applaud you, My child, because you do. Continue to sing praises to My Name as you share and introduce Me to others.

I also applaud you for being available to Me. You are free to be and to do whatever I want. Thank you for hearing and listening to Me and for not returning to your job. You are correct when you say, "I now work for the Lord." Continue to avail yourself in your one-on-one time with Me. Continue to remind yourself that I Am your Source and that I shall compensate you. Lock your eyes on Me and follow Me closely. Adhere to what I shall show you. You know Me to be the Way, not the how, but the Way. Yes, I Am the Way, and I shall lead and guide you to lead others along the way.

Your Thoughts or Prayer

_____

_____

_____

_____

_____

_____

_____

_____

_____

_____

_____

_____

_____

_____

_____

_____

_____

_____

_____

_____

DAY EIGHT

Do pause to listen to My voice and to hear Me whenever you have prayed to Me. I love responding to you. Remember that prayer is talking to Me and listening to Me. Once again, thank you for singing praises to My Name. You sang My Name is:

1—Almighty	10—Just	19—Savior
2—Blesser	11—Keeper	20—Trust
3—Committed	12—Light	21—Understanding
4—Dedicated	13—Mercy	22—Vivacious
5—Everything	14—Nice	23—Wonderful
6—Forgiveness	15—Opulent	24—X-extra
7—Grace	16—Propitiation	25—Yahweh
8—Hearer	17—Quiet	26—Zestful
9—Inspirational	18—Richness	

Thank you for letting Me know who you know Me to be. I desire to be all of that and more of Who I Am in you. The more of Me you take on, the more you are imitating Me. The more you imitate Me, the brighter your light will be for Me. That, My child, is the way you let your light so shine to draw others to Me. So be the light, My child. Look for opportunities to shine My light upon others. Go ahead and give them love, which is Me. Go ahead, be the light, love/God them. Give them Me, God.

Your Thoughts or Prayer

_____

_____

_____

_____

_____

_____

_____

_____

_____

_____

_____

_____

_____

_____

_____

_____

_____

_____

DAY NINE

Yes, I called you My child when you told Me about your age during this morning's prayer time. No matter what number your age is, you will always be My child, Mine, My child, you are. As My child, you have childlike faith, and you can trust Me. As My child, not only can you trust Me, but you can also obey Me. Not only can you obey Me, but you can also walk with Me.

You can walk together with Me as you did with your earthly father. Picture yourself holding his hand with no resistance or fear. You knew that you were safe because you were with your daddy. That is how I wish all My children would feel about Me daily. How I wish they would have the childlike faith to trust Me. I want them to know that because their hand is in My hand, there is no reason for them to be fearful and not to trust Me. Your hand, My child, remained in your earthly daddy's hands as long as you wanted to. You never heard him say, "I am tired of holding your hand; let go of mine." You and a few others know that about Me. I would never tell you to let go of My hand. Yes, My child, if only all My children would just put their hand in My hand, fearlessly walk with Me, trust Me, and journey with Me.

Your Thoughts or Prayer

_____

_____

_____

_____

_____

_____

_____

_____

_____

_____

_____

_____

_____

_____

_____

_____

_____

_____

_____

DAY TEN

It shall always be My delight and My pleasure to hear you sing praises to My Name. As you know, there is no name greater than My Name. As the songwriter says, "There's nobody greater than You."

I see that your list this morning was a bit limited in alphabetically describing My Name. It's okay, My child. The more you sit quietly and meditate on My Name, the more you will be able to fill in the blanks. What's really important is that you and others know Who I Am. It's the "I Am" who you see and experience:

I Am He who sits on the throne with all power. I Am the true living God.

I Am your Righteousness. I Am your Father.

I Am your Maker. I Am your Healer.

I Am your constant Companion and your very best Friend.

I Am your Peace. I Am your Comforter.

I Am your Deliverer. I Am your Refuge and your Strong Tower.

I Am your Keeper. I Am your Joy.

I Am your all in all, your anything and everything you need Me to be. It's the I Am of My Name. It blesses Me, My child, that you not only know My Name but that you know Who I Am. I Am no stranger to you. You know that you can always trust The Great I Am, not the "I Was" nor the "I Will," but The Great I Am Who is always present.

Your Thoughts or Prayer

_____

_____

_____

_____

_____

_____

_____

_____

_____

_____

_____

_____

_____

_____

_____

_____

_____

DAY ELEVEN

I see that your mind is all over the place. What excites Me the most about it is that your mind is on Me like you are trying to see through My eyes what the world and the Body of Christ look like.

As you can see, My people have made a mess of things. Instead of letting their lights shine, they have set aside their lamps and wallowed in the dimness of the darkness. They have gotten such a glimpse of the world and its glittering, colorful lights that they have put the real light aside. They have forgotten that I Am the brightest Light. I Am the Light.

I Am the Light that they seek for any set of circumstances they face. My light is the way and the only light that dispels darkness. They are fascinated by the hues of bright red, yellow, orange, blue, etc. Those lights do entertain and tantalize (excite the senses or desires of someone by definition). Those lights can never lead the way to the Truth that shall set them free to become all that they desire to become and, more importantly, free to become all that I desire for them to be. I Am the Light, My child.

I Am the only real light that can set the captives free. So, imitate Me, My child, as you draw nearer to Me. Let My light shine through you so that those in darkness can see My light through you and let My light shine through them. No light in this world is brighter or more beautiful than Me, The Great I Am.

∽

Your Thoughts or Prayer

_____

_____

_____

_____

_____

_____

_____

_____

_____

_____

_____

_____

_____

DAY TWELVE

You have blessed Me by far with your "concert," as you called it. Yes, My child, I love for you to sing praises about My Name. This morning you sang praises to Me. What a delight to hear you sing. I delight in you singing songs from days of old, which says to Me how sensitive you are to the leading of My Spirit. It is Me who is bringing back to your memory those songs that you sang during yesteryear. You don't remember when or where you learned those songs. I shall continue to bring them to your re-membrance. You are truly worshipping Me in Spirit and in Truth. I Am perfecting your voice as you sing. Do not tell others that you cannot sing. Remember, you can do all things through Christ, Who strengthens you. It only takes a yielded and willing heart to do what pleases Me. How I Wish My people would sing to Me more and more.

I Am perfecting that which concerns you. Would I neglect your voice and your ability to sing when I know that it is the desire of your heart to have the gift of singing? Yes, My child, I Am perfecting your gift of singing as you delight yourself in Me.

Your Thoughts or Prayer

_____

_____

_____

_____

_____

_____

_____

_____

_____

_____

_____

_____

_____

_____

_____

_____

_____

_____

_____

_____

Day Thirteen

Once again, thank you for delighting Me with your presence and singing, which puts a smile on My face and in My heart. You said that you were reminded of how you would go to see your grandmother. You didn't go to get anything from her. You went to take her joy and smiles. You have done the same for Me. I can hear that song singing in your inward parts, "All I Want Is You." That pleases Me to the utmost.

Now, I have the liberty to fill you with more of Me. Words nor imagination can fathom all of what I desire to give you. My favor shall rest upon your shoulders, My child. I delight in giving you more of Me. Know that the more of Me I give to you, the more of Me you shall desire, and the more you shall be filled to function out of My overflow. The brighter your light will shine as more of My Glory shines through you. Yes, My child, I shall fill you with My Glory, overflowing.

Your Thoughts or Prayer

_____

_____

_____

_____

_____

_____

_____

_____

_____

_____

_____

_____

_____

_____

_____

_____

_____

_____

_____

_____

DAY FOURTEEN

I hear and feel the heaviness of your heart. If your concerns are grievous to you, how much more grievous to Me, The Great I Am Who sits high and sees low! I see everything and everyone, My child, and My heart is breaking. I long for the lost and those who have turned their backs to Me. There are those who are lukewarm, straddling the fence, and totally non-committal to the cause of Christ. Now that COVID-19 has prevented them from attending the church building, they have little and no desire to read My Word or to pray. Spending time with Me is the last thing on their daily agenda (if I Am on their agenda at all).

They act as though they are smarter than I. They act as though they do not believe that apart from Me, they can do nothing. They do not believe that I Am faithful in all My Ways.

Some of My people don't believe that I Am Who I say that I Am. They do not realize that I have the perfect plan for their life. They doubt if I Am the Way, the Truth, and the Life. They don't think about going to heaven because their focus is on getting through this world-system life.

They have no respect for Me and My timing. Many have taken on the stance: "Forget God. I am tired of waiting on Him. I am tired of going through changes, trying to make sense of what's going on and what to do. So, I am done with God." I Am so very pleased to have My remnant of people who are holding fast and holding on to Me. The effectual fervent prayers of the righteous shall avail much. So pray, My child, and pray without ceasing for My people and for the lost. Yes, My child, I Am coming back, and I shall return soon!

❧

Your Thoughts or Prayer

_____

_____

_____

_____

_____

_____

_____

_____

DAY FIFTEEN

Thank you for inviting Me into your presence. Many of My children do not take time to spend with Me. It's like the neglect that the elderly experience. People are so busy doing themselves that they forget to do Me, God.

You, My child, are learning to seek Me, and I welcome you. I applaud you, and I shall reward you. I know that you are appreciative and excited about just being in My Presence. Did I not promise that I would give you the desires of your heart, simply if you would delight yourself in Me?

Delighting yourself in Me is more of an action than a feeling. It's like love. Many see love as a deep or great feeling. To love and to delight oneself is a yielding of self, your entire being to Me. As you give more and more of yourself to Me, you should receive more and more of Me. Did I not promise to give back to you "good measure, pressed down, shaken together, and running over"?

So, thank you, My child, for pouring yourself out to Me through your songs of adoration. Thank you, My child, for gracing Me with your presence. Also, thank you for inviting Me into your presence. I feel welcomed, appreciated, and honored.

Love and delight are a two-way street, an exchange. It started at Calvary when I became the Propitiation. I took on your debt, and you took on My life. I died for you. You get to live in Me and for Me. It's the win-win effect of an unselfish love from Me to you and vice-versa.

I have enjoyed your worship and your presence this morning, My dear one. Now you shall be able to enjoy My Presence and delight yourself in Me. That is what true intimacy is about, you in-to-Me. Because you are in-to-Me, I shall manifest Myself in-to-you. So, be in Me as I Am in you.

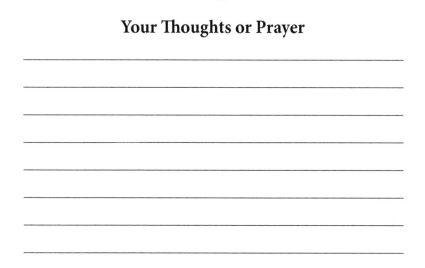

Your Thoughts or Prayer

_____

_____

_____

_____

_____

_____

_____

Day Sixteen

Good morning, My child. I delight to fellowship with you again. Thank you for coming to hear from Me before falling asleep. Falling asleep in My Presence is a subtle work of the enemy. Yes, My child, I know you were disappointed. Disappointment does not come from Me, as you know. Disappointment comes because of your expectancy. The only One Who will not disappoint you is Me. Disappointment is expectancy in something or someone other than Me.

As you know, I will not fail you. I shall always encourage you. So, when you experience disappointment, check the source of it. Was it Me? Sometimes you set yourself up for disappointment because you are expecting your plan to work out. If your plan doesn't work out, that was not My plan for you. Sometimes you expect certain others to give you affirmation on a project or an idea of yours, and it's a letdown when they don't.

Bear in mind that I Am your Source. All blessings flow from Me, not others, even though I may bless you through others. Whenever you get an idea from Me, receive it and wait on Me to bring it to pass. Many people are dream killers because they have not seen Me move in certain ways. They are not open to Me doing things differently or creatively. So, when I give you an idea, sit on it quietly and wait for Me to bring it into fruition. I Am the Creator of infinite possibilities. Trust Me with what you are hearing and thinking. Dare to dream, and dream big, My child. Whenever someone speaks doubt on what I have given you, pray for their insight and their willingness to be receptive to new things.

Keep your focus on Me. Keep listening, hearing, and recording what you are hearing. Trust Me with all your heart. Keep doubt out of your heart. Doubt, like disappointment and fear, is not of Me. Trust Me, My child, and get validation from only Me. Act on everything you hear and trust Me for the outcome. Now, go and write that letter. Send it upon completion of your project. I will let you know when. Be encouraged, not discouraged, My child. I Am the God of infinite possibilities.

Your Thoughts or Prayer

_____

_____

_____

_____

_____

_____

_____

_____

_____

_____

_____

_____

_____

_____

_____

_____

_____

_____

_____

_____

_____

_____

Day Seventeen

Good morning, My child. I delight to be in your presence and to hear you sing praises to Me. Thank you for not only inviting Me but for welcoming Me as well. I delight in joining you.

You were reminded of the time you experienced the loss of your dear friend. You felt like you were floating on a blanket in midair. It was my blanket of comfort, My child. You were pained too much to go through that trauma. So, I carried you.

It would take you these many years later to experience that blanket ride again. The difference is there is no trauma attached to it. It's my free carpet ride of comfort. I delight to have you ride with Me. Your heart is so open to Me.

Your heart is so turned to Me. Your heart is so open to Me. I delight in filling your heart with Me. When your heart is filled with Me, there is no lack. You are now equipped to pour out to others what I have poured into You, My child. You are filled with My love, My peace, and My joy. As I give it to you, simply pass it on. Be sensitive to the needs of those whom I bring across your path. I have shed My love abroad in your heart to share it with others.

Your Thoughts or Prayer

_____

_____

_____

_____

_____

_____

_____

_____

_____

_____

_____

_____

_____

_____

_____

_____

_____

_____

Day Eighteen

Good morning, My child. Once again, I Am delighted to fellowship with you this morning while it is still dark, in the quiet of this new day. Thank you for your songs of praise to Me.

You have noticed and realized the great exchange, My dear, and it starts with Me. For every move I make, for every action I take, and for everything I give, there is an opposite exchange for you. I died so that you can live. I, the Propitiation, took on sin so that you would not have to deal with the power and penalty of sin. When I come back, I will eradicate the presence of sin. As you know, sin cannot last.

As for more the exchange, I give you Me, and you freely accept Me as your Savior and Lord. I give you My Word, and you receive My daily bread. I give you access to My throne, and you receive My grace and mercy. I give you eternal life, and you receive My Presence forever.

Your Thoughts or Prayer

_____

_____

_____

_____

_____

_____

_____

_____

_____

_____

_____

_____

_____

_____

_____

_____

_____

_____

_____

_____

Day Nineteen

Your list of thanks to Me this morning has made Me glad, glad that you are appreciative of Who I Am and of what I have done in and through you. I delight to do more, My child, and I shall.

You now realize that the essence of living is loving, and the essence of loving is giving. You are correct when you refer to the Great Exchange. The essence of giving is emptying yourself and receiving all of Me. As a result, you shall become all of who I have made you be.

Thank you, My child, for your desire to sup with Me daily by way of your purposeful efforts to come to talk with Me. Thank you for opening your ears and your heart to hear from Me.

∽

Your Thoughts or Prayer

_____

_____

_____

_____

_____

Day Twenty

Once again, here is to thank you for coming to sup with Me. I look forward to your daily visitations. There is no forced coercion, and as you mentioned, you have not come to take anything from Me. You have come just to spend time with Me as did Jesus, according to Mark 1:35. That blesses Me. You can imagine the joy it brings to My heart, My child. Yes, this is the desire that I wish more of My children would genuinely have of Me, just to be here with Me and not to take anything from Me.

I will give them their hearts' desires just because I already know what they need, and I anticipate and provide their needs accordingly. Imagine how you feel if a person comes to visit with you only to get something from you because they know that you are a giver. You would prefer that they not come to visit with you with wrong and selfish motives. So, thank you, My child, for your effortless and purposeful desire to do as Jesus did, wake up early in the morning while it was yet dark to sup with Me.

Yes, the table is set, and I have prepared a place setting for you. You are curious about My Word that says, "...prepare a table before Me in the presence of mine enemies." Whoever are the enemies that are lurching like leeches upon you, they must fall off like dead flies because they cannot remain in My Presence. So, just by coming before My Presence, you are receiving blood washing and purification. The more you are in My Presence, the more your light shall shine. Shine bright for Me. Be the light!

$\sim\!\!\infty\!\!\sim$

Your Thoughts or Prayer

_____

_____

_____

_____

_____

_____

_____

_____

_____

_____

_____

_____

Day Twenty-One

Thank you for delighting Me with your presence once again. As usual, I have enjoyed your singing in your natural language and in your prayer language. I do desire to abide in the presence of My people.

Be anxious for nothing, for I have overcome everything that concerns you personally and the world. I am allowing you to hear and see what I hear and see daily. As things affect you negatively, do not faint in your heart. Instead, use these weighty concerns as immediate prayer needs. You may wonder if this is your imagination, your sensitivity, or is it real. You don't have to figure it out. Just surrender those concerns to Me. I will respond to whatever you give to me because I Am concerned about everything that concerns you. Listen to your heart, your emotions, and your suspicions. Commit those things to Me, and I will attend to them accordingly. Remember that you are standing in the gap on behalf of others. I delight in going to bat for you. In other words, I delight in responding to your prayers. So, pray on, My child.

Your Thoughts or Prayer

_____

_____

_____

_____

_____

_____

_____

_____

_____

_____

_____

_____

_____

_____

_____

_____

_____

_____

_____

_____

Day Twenty-Two

Thank you for coming before My Presence to sing praises and to worship Me this morning. You truly make My heart smile and sing. As you sang "I'll Never Know How Much It Cost to See My Sins Upon the Cross," I just want you to know it was worth it. Every drop of blood was costly to pay for the price of your sins and the sins of the entire world. If I had to do it again, yes, I would do it again. Not everyone will receive Me or accept Me as Savior and Lord, but it is so worth it for whosoever will.

My child, I delight to be the Savior of the world. I love My Creation, oh so much. It is My desire that My entire creation will live forever with Me where there is no pain, no darkness, and no suffering at all. It shall be like regaining My garden of Eden with its perfect conditions. The only difference shall be that My garden will be full of many, many people and not just the first two. I Am coming back for all who want to be with Me, in the garden of endless love, joy, and peace.

Your Thoughts or Prayer

_____
_____
_____
_____
_____
_____
_____
_____
_____
_____
_____
_____
_____
_____
_____
_____
_____
_____
_____
_____
_____

Day Twenty-Three

Know, My child, that I Am so very pleased with the praises I have heard from you this morning. What a benevolent offering you have given Me! I delight to be in your presence because you have most definitely ushered Me in. That is how I Am invited into your presence, My child, with heart-felt praises. One song right after another just flowed from your heart. Thank you for pouring out your heart to Me. I receive each praise and every breath you poured out to Me. That is what I call "perfect" praise, and you are to be commended.

So, you see, not only do you respond to my request that you come before My Presence with praise and thanksgiving, but I come before your presence because your praise has ushered Me in your presence. It's that exchange again. As you do for Me and to Me, I shall do for you and to you. Thank you, My child, for your perfect heartfelt praise this morning. Not only do you honor Me, but I also honor you. Enter My rest. Empty yourself of any anxiety and bask in My Presence all day long. With you, I Am well pleased.

Your Thoughts or Prayer

_____

_____

_____

_____

_____

_____

_____

_____

_____

_____

_____

_____

_____

_____

_____

_____

_____

_____

_____

_____

_____

Day Twenty-Four

I am delighted to be in your presence, and as usual, I have enjoyed your singing to Me. As you sing praises to Me, it says to Me that you esteem Me highly, and truly there is no one greater in your eyesight. I Am high and lifted up and greater than anyone or anything. That's why you can sing:

- "I sing Praises to Your (My) Name"
- "There's Nobody Greater/Couldn't Find Nobody Greater Than Me"
- "God's Worthy, He's Worthy, Almighty Creator, Alpha, Omega, Beginning, and the End"
- "Hallelujah, Hallelujah."

As you:

A) Praise Me	D) Glorify Me	G) Give thanks to Me
B) Worship Me	E) Magnify Me	H) Lay down your life to Me
C) Honor Me	F) Serve Me	I) Live for Me

And then you sang "Welcome into This Place," welcoming Me into you, the broken vessel. Yes, I desire to abide in the praises of My people who lift their hands and offer praise unto My Name. Yes, My child, I feel very welcomed into your place, into the center or core of your being, in your heart. I delight in abiding there as you delight in singing praises unto Me and unto My Name. Sing, My child, sing unto Me.

Your Thoughts or Prayer

_____

_____

_____

_____

_____

_____

_____

_____

_____

_____

_____

_____

_____

_____

_____

_____

_____

_____

Day Twenty-Five

I can hear you singing "You Are Welcome" over and over. It blesses Me because I know that it is true. In your heart, you are welcoming Me to abide in your praises. Where else can I abide but in your heart? Thank you so much, My child. Yes, indeed, I desire to abide in the praises of My people.

Thank you for responding to My early morning wake-up. With a bit less than five hours of sleep, you hastened to My call. You didn't contemplate nor hesitate; you simply woke up and got up. It says to Me that your sensitivity to My early morning nudging is becoming more real and apparent. You are harkening to My small, soft voice. The cry of My call is to wake up! That is what I want My people to do, simply wake up.

Even when My People eventually wake up physically, far too many are spiritually sleeping in My Presence. They are being carried by their own whims. If they wake up to Me daily, they would be sensitive to My voice and to My lead. Until they become more sensitive to My lead, they will lack living in and experiencing the blessings of being in My Presence where there is the fullness of

My love, joy, and peace. Welcome, My dear, into My Presence.

Your Thoughts or Prayer

_____

_____

_____

_____

_____

_____

_____

_____

_____

_____

_____

_____

_____

_____

_____

_____

_____

_____

_____

Day Twenty-Six

It blesses Me that you were sensitive to My touch and arose to commune with Me even after only three hours of sleep. You could have asked for more sleep time, and I would have granted it, but as you said, you desire to sacrifice your sleep and meet with Me instead of turning over as you have sometimes in the past.

Sacrificing your sleep is another opportunity to die to yourself and to demonstrate your love, sensitivity, and your obedience to Me, My child. You shall be rewarded for your sacrifice and obedience. My rewards are not always what you can see. As you know, according to 2 Corinthians 4:18 (NIV), "We fix our eyes not on what is seen, but on what is unseen..." The real things are the invisible things. Anything that you can see is temporary.

Do not be anxious about the needs of your loved ones. Thank you for bringing them to Me in prayer. I've got them as I have you. Did I not say, "Be anxious for nothing?" I shall have My perfect way with them and My perfect way with you. I do not overlook nor leave anything undone.

I Am God. I Am God Who sees all, knows all, and watches over all. By the way, your songs of praise did not go unnoticed or unappreciated. I love when you and My people sing praises to Me and My Name. Can't you see and hear the angels singing twenty-four-seven, "Holy, holy, holy to the Lord, God Almighty?"

"I AM Who I AM." You may now go back to sleep.

⸎

Your Thoughts or Prayer

_____

_____

_____

_____

_____

_____

_____

_____

_____

_____

_____

_____

Day Twenty-Seven

Your mind is like a racehorse this morning. It is all over the place. I speak My peace over you. Have I not said to be anxious for nothing, but with prayer and thanksgiving, make your request known to Me? And because I know all things, I already know what your heart desires. You also know Me to be faithful. Great is My faithfulness. Take delight that I Am Omniscient, and I Am Omnipotent. All power is in My hands, and I Am indeed everywhere present. Absolutely nothing takes place unless it is orchestrated by Me. There is no need to wonder why I allow whatever I allow. My plans for mankind were made before the foundation of the world. Trust whatever I allow to befall you and whatever I allow to happen around you. Again, there is never a need to be anxious about them.

So, I bid you to exercise your childlike faith and to walk in your big shoes. Walk tall in them, and walk with Me, in time and in step. Trust where I Am leading you and what I shall allow to happen. Remember My Promises. Have I not promised to be near you, to walk with you, to protect you, to forgive you, to heal you, to sustain you, to never leave you, and to come back for you? Is there a gap in My Promises, My child? Am I lacking in any area? Remember that doubt and fear are never of Me or from Me. So, go in peace, My child, with your childlike faith, trusting Me all the way. Be anxious for nothing. Peace, be still!

Your Thoughts or Prayer

_____

_____

_____

_____

_____

_____

_____

_____

_____

_____

_____

_____

_____

Day Twenty-Eight

Have I not said be anxious for nothing? I Am going to use your mouthpiece this morning, and I recognize how jittery you are. Do not try to prepare an introduction, just open your mouth and trust Me to speak through you. Trust Me with your childlike faith. As you know, I Am never sleeping or slumbering. I Am very aware of what I want to say through you. Thank you for studying and preparing for this moment.

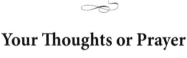

Your Thoughts or Prayer

_____

_____

_____

_____

_____

_____

_____

_____

_____

_____

DAY TWENTY-NINE

One of the reasons you keep falling asleep this morning during prayer time with Me is because you have not gotten enough sleep. The enemy will do everything and anything to prevent you from concentrating on Me. Thank you for continuing to press.

∽

Your Thoughts or Prayer

_____

_____

_____

_____

_____

_____

_____

_____

_____

_____

_____

DAY THIRTY

I applaud you for your intense desire to come and commune with Me. Your tongues flowed frequently and fluidly, yet you succumbed to sleep.

You experienced a crazy dream. I want you to pray for the person you saw in your dreams. She needs prayer and a closer walk with Me.

You also saw another person. She was very glad to see you. She is very lonely, but she doesn't know how to reach out. She tries to handle things alone. She's not really connected to a church, but she does go to church. Call her today.

The church you attend is full of people, but it is not full of Me. As you could see when you were going to the restroom, there were very many people and much chatter outside the sanctuary during the service. Sadly, too many of My people go to church to see and hear from other people instead of Me. Pray for the churchgoers who are not going to church for the right reasons.

Your Thoughts or Prayer

DAY THIRTY-ONE

You did a wonderful job of praying in your prayer language. It says to Me that your spirit was yielded to My Holy Spirit. Know that exactly what you prayed for was led by My Spirit and not by you. Know also that you have been edified and built up in Me.

Thank you for your obedience yesterday, for calling the person who I told you to call, and for praying for the other person who needs prayer. Continue to pray for them as often as they cross your mind. You will be yielding to the prompting and leading of My Holy Spirit.

Having talked with the person who I have instructed you to call is confirmation that you are indeed hearing from Me. So, erase any doubt that it is Me speaking and not yourself. Doubt and fear shall constantly attempt to creep in. You must cast them down immediately.

Do you recall feeling My Presence as you spoke to that person and how that person quieted himself, listened, and agreed? You told that person that it was a "God moment." Thank You for giving Me credit and the glory. Know that I love you, and with you, I Am well pleased.

Your Thoughts or Prayer

_____

_____

_____

_____

_____

_____

_____

_____

_____

_____

_____

_____

_____

_____

_____

_____

_____

_____

_____

Day Thirty-Two

Thank you for getting up and coming before My Presence. Even though it's a bit later than usual, you are still purposing to sup with Me and to edify yourself by use of your prayer language.

As you sang "Here I Am to Worship," it was beautiful music to my ears. "I Am Who I Am." It blesses Me when you acknowledge The Great I Am that I Am.

Your thoughts are swiftly fleeting about the things concerning your book. You are to share the purposes of the book, which are for the reader to:

1. Hear what I, God, have spoken.
2. Meditate on what I have said.
3. Write down what he/she heard.
4. Write about how what I said relates to the reader.
5. Write a plan of application pertaining to what I said.

This shall ultimately strengthen the reader's discipline of listening for My voice after praying to Me. He/she shall become more intimately acquainted with "Who I Am" as the Heavenly Father and what I, Father God, said.

Your Thoughts or Prayer

_____

_____

_____

_____

_____

_____

_____

_____

_____

_____

_____

_____

_____

_____

_____

_____

_____

_____

_____

_____

_____

_____

_____

Day Thirty-Three

Your heart is so very yielded to Me. I applaud and thank you for your willingness to lay your all on the altar this morning. You said, "Your all is Mine to do whatever I want to do with it."

Yes, My child, the cry of My heart is that all My children will get to the place of putting their all, all of themselves on My altar of love. I will give back to them the purest of hearts so that they can represent Me more beautifully on this earth realm. The purer one is, the brighter their light shines. The brighter their light shines, the more others can see Me, Jesus. Only then will the masses be drawn to Me. It's My Light among men that they can see, which shall be the Light that draws them and points them to the Way. Yes, My child, I Am the Way. All must and can only come to the Father by Way of Me.

I Am the open door that leads all who are willing to follow The Great I Am. He is waiting so patiently for all the who-so-ever to come. If only they would rid themselves of the resistance that prevents them from following close after Me. Was this not the cry from the very beginning to make room for Me so that I may take all to the Promised Land where The Great I Am lives?

Know that He lives within the heart of every man who has given his/her heart to me. Only a few have opened their hearts wide to receive more of Me. The more of Me they receive, the more like Me they become. I have spoken. Let the church say, "Amen, amen," and "Selah." So be it!

Your Thoughts or Prayer

_____

_____

_____

_____

_____

_____

_____

_____

_____

_____

_____

DAY THIRTY-FOUR

I am so very pleased with how you yielded yourself to Me and how you spoke of Me. You gave My people hope and encouragement to keep looking to Me, the Author and Finisher of their faith. Know that as you continue to spend time in My Word, in prayer, and in My Presence, I shall be your mouthpiece. I shall speak through you, and I shall sing through you. I ask only for your availability and for you to yield yourself to Me. How else can I use one as an instrument of My Righteousness if he/she is too busy to spend time with Me? It's in My Presence you communicate and interact with The Great I Am:

I Am all you need
I Am your Sufficiency
I Am your Answer
I Am your Solution to every problem

Can you think of anything that I Am not? I Am committed to doing for you whatever is needed. Thank you for acknowledging Me as the Master with every Master Plan. Yes, I Am Father, God, Who knows best and Who knows all. Thank you, My child, for your companionship.

Your Thoughts or Prayer

_____

_____

_____

_____

_____

_____

_____

_____

_____

_____

_____

_____

_____

_____

_____

_____

_____

_____

_____

_____

_____

Day Thirty-Five

Your desire to be like Me is indeed a blessing. That is what oneness is all about. As I, the Father, and Jesus are one, so are you desirous of being in oneness with Us, in alignment with Us. That means that you desire to think like Me, the I Am. You desire to talk like Me. You desire to operate like Me in the earth. What a great representative and representation of Me you shall be! That is how you rise and shine and let your light shine for Me for the world to see. It is the radiance of the bright light that will draw mankind out of the darkness.

Remember the world was dark, the Holy Spirit hovered over the darkness, and I said, "Let there be light." The light was the beginning of My Creation. Your light to others will dispel the darkness in others and enable them to become new creations in Me. As a light dispenser, you shall be like Me, creating something good and beautiful. So, be the light and shine bright. Let them see Me, the light in you. Be the light like Jesus. Thank you for co-laboring with Me, helping to build My Kingdom.

Your Thoughts or Prayer

_____

_____

_____

_____

_____

_____

_____

_____

_____

_____

_____

_____

_____

_____

_____

_____

_____

_____

_____

_____

_____

_____

_____

DAY THIRTY-SIX

Your mind is racing like a racehorse. It's all over the place. I do understand that you have at least three things before you get done. Anxiety is trying to creep in. Doubt, fear, and worry are not of Me, so put an end to your anxiety. Focus on first things first. Need I remind you of Who is first? Yes, of course, I Am first. So cast all your concerns on Me right now.

Thank you for the song, My child, "I Cast All of My Cares upon You." Now, allow My peace to cover you like a warm, soft blanket. Just breathe comfortably and allow Me, the Holy Spirit, to lead and guide you. Is that not who I Am? I Am He, the Holy Spirit, Who leads and guides you to do whatever needs to get done. Without coming first to Me, you do it in your own strengths. By turning first to Me, it gets done in My Strength. Which is greater, your strength or Mine?

Your Thoughts or Prayer

_____

_____

_____

_____

_____

_____

_____

_____

_____

_____

_____

_____

_____

_____

_____

_____

_____

_____

_____

Day Thirty-Seven

I enjoyed your worship song this morning, "I'll Love You Forever and Forever." Yes, My child, it is the cry of My heart that My children will love Me, and not only love Me but love Me forever.

Can't you imagine or see the angels singing "Holy, Holy, Holy" to Me as they continuously worship and honor Me? To hear My children sing I love You is indeed music to My ears. No matter how much they or you love Me, I will always love you even more, simply because I Am Love. Love comes from no other direction or no other source. It begins and ends with Me. As you know, with Me, there is no end.

I hear the sighs and cries of your heart, My child. Trust Me to protect you. As you know and have often declared, "I Am The Great I Am Who knows all things." Trust Me to protect you, My child, from any accusations that may come your way. Just stand still and watch Me cover you and protect you. Now, go in peace. Thank you for your honesty. I shall vindicate you.

Your Thoughts or Prayer

_____

_____

_____

_____

_____

_____

_____

_____

_____

_____

_____

_____

_____

_____

_____

_____

_____

_____

_____

_____

_____

_____

DAY THIRTY-EIGHT

You have heard Me correctly. I want truth in the inward parts. Too few of My people have humbled themselves, yet they are asking Me to do this and to do that for them. Many are victims of self-righteousness. Many are so okay with themselves. They have accepted Me as Savior; they know how to pray; they know many scriptures, and they have been "churchy" for days. Unfortunately, they don't know what is truly lurking within their own heart, primarily because they are fearful of looking.

Have I not said that men love darkness more than light? It's the covering that they desire to keep. "If I don't let this cat out of the bag, if I can keep these skeletons covered in my closet," they say to themselves, "no one has to know." They have buried those dark secrets, which are packed into chests and suitcases with locks and signs. The keys have been thrown away, and the signs are saying, "Do not disturb," not ever to be opened again.

They want to be the light. How can they be light with so much darkness compacted and buried on the inside? Yes, my dear, I

Am coming for Truth on the inside and on the inward parts. I will not quit knocking on the doors of their hearts until they have finally surrendered their hidden to Me. I Am the Light that shall expose and dispel the darkness on the inside of My people so that they will be free to rid themselves of all their darkness and dark secrets. Each dark secret must be removed so that they can truly worship Me in Spirit and in Truth.

Your Thoughts or Prayer

_____

_____

_____

_____

_____

_____

_____

_____

_____

_____

_____

_____

DAY THIRTY-NINE

I visit My remnant to remind them that I Am with them. My Presence is the greatest gift one could have on earth. My Presence is My Gift to you. I delight in saturating you with My Presence. Here's confirmation that, in My Presence, there is fullness of joy—joy to overflowing. May it carry you through this season of acknowledging and recognizing "Who I AM." I Am He, the Light of the world.

∽↝

Your Thoughts or Prayer

_____

_____

_____

_____

_____

_____

_____

_____

_____

_____

Day Forty

Your heart is carrying your loved ones and your pastor's concerns. You feel the weightiness of their situations. Know that I Am their Carrier because I Am able. I have the strength to carry them all. Not only am I carrying them, but I Am also comforting them. I am the Comforter of all who will allow Me to be.

Too often, My people retreat to their hiding places instead of retreating to Me as if I Am not their refuge—their very present help in time of need and trouble. Do not try to carry their loads. Thank you for bringing their names and concerns to Me. Such is the heart of an intercessor, feeling the heaviness of others and bringing them to Me in prayer. Rest in the assurance that My heart is tender towards them and their needs. I shall carry their loads. I shall carry them during their temporary season of heaviness. Now that you have brought them to Me, release their weight. Continue to pray for them as you are led or prompted by My Holy Spirit.

Your Thoughts or Prayer

_____

_____

_____

_____

_____

_____

_____

_____

_____

_____

_____

_____

_____

_____

_____

_____

_____

_____

_____

_____

_____

_____

DAY FORTY-ONE

Thank you for singing praises to Me. Yes, I Am Jesus, Righteous, Worthy, and Holy.

I Am the One Who sits upon the throne.

In My Presence are peace, joy, and love. Do you not feel all three in the atmosphere?

Can you think of anything better to possess and experience on any given day? You, My dear, have found the secret and/or answer to having a victorious God-given day. It is Me, The Great I Am, Who is your love, joy, and peace. There is no other source. If only others will awaken a simple desire to sing praises to Me and to allow My Spirit to speak to their hearts and minds. I have just ordered Your day as you continue to purpose to come first to Me. The fulfillment of My Promise to add everything else shall be granted daily because it is Me Whom you should seek first (see Matthew 6:34).

Your Thoughts or Prayer

_____

_____

_____

_____

_____

_____

_____

_____

_____

_____

_____

_____

_____

_____

_____

_____

_____

_____

_____

_____

_____

_____

_____

DAY FORTY-TWO

Know that I hear, heard, and know the cry and the desires of your heart. Did I not only say and promise to give you the desires of your heart if you delight yourself in Me? You, My child, have indeed delighted and saturated your desires in Me. They shall be granted. I delight in giving you the platform to become and to do all of what your heart desires to promote My Kingdom because you recognize that it is not for you to get the glory.

Yes, My child, because you love Me, you want to do the simple things I have asked. Feed My sheep, make disciples, point all men unto Me, and not to yourself.

The mistake that far too many of My pastors, elders, bishops, apostles, teachers, and leaders make is that they tend to encourage My people to depend on themselves instead of teaching them to depend on Me. I know that you are among the few whom I can trust to encourage My people to depend on Me. I Am a jealous God, and no man will share My Glory.

It is Me Who makes all things happen. Keep your focus only on Me as you watch how others quietly steal My Glory, some-times unknowingly, sometimes knowingly. Remember, the heart of man is deceitful and desperately wicked. Who can know it but I? Only I, The Great I Am, Who knows all and sees all. Keep your eyes on Me, My child. I shall show you great and mighty things because I know that I can trust you and your pure heart.

∽∾

Your Thoughts or Prayer

_____

_____

_____

_____

_____

_____

_____

_____

_____

_____

_____

_____

DAY FORTY-THREE

Once again, you have graced Me with your presence, like Jesus, while it was yet dark. Thank you for purposing to come before My Presence for no other reason but because you simply want to. There is no pressure, you are not in pain or hurt, and you do not have a situation from which you are begging Me to deliver you. You have simply come to commune with Me. Oh, how you have blessed Me! I am delighted to meet with you, just the two of us.

Can you not feel My Peace, My child? Can you not feel the quietness and the stillness of this morning? Many people have no idea how loud the quietness and stillness of a day can be because they do not choose to seek Me early, like Jesus did in Mark 1:35, early in the morning while it was dark. These are the golden hours of the morning in which My remnant experiences the quiet of the morning of each day. Enjoy it, My child, if you can because soon the sounds of all varieties shall crowd out the quiet. So, in the meantime, continue this blessed quietness with Me.

Thank you for meeting with Me in the quiet of this new day, and thank you for giving yourself to Me to allow Me to order your day. Yes, I have the Master Plan for your day today because I Am the Master. More importantly, I Am your Master. Sit still in the quiet and just be.

∽

Your Thoughts or Prayer

_____

_____

_____

_____

_____

_____

_____

_____

_____

_____

_____

_____

_____

DAY FORTY-FOUR

I Am allowing you to walk alongside your loved one to be aware of what can take place within a family when the deceased one has not left their affairs in order. You are to encourage your loved ones to "get their house in order" just in case their untimely death is left in your hands. As you know, I Am a God of order. If My people purpose to do all things in order, there would be no need for verbal arguments, which are sure to follow.

It is very important that a will is written so that all parties involved will know what is to be done with the personal belongings that are left behind. Allow all parties to write their own letters outlining how personal property is to be distributed. Then, come together to share, and do not argue. A person has a right to distribute their property the way they prefer, whether it's to another's liking or not. Acceptance of where another's heart is key. Do not procrastinate. As you know, death can be sudden. Sit down together and share your will with your most significant others to make them aware of your wishes and vice versa.

Your Thoughts or Prayer

_____

_____

_____

_____

_____

_____

_____

_____

_____

_____

_____

_____

_____

_____

_____

_____

_____

_____

_____

_____

_____

_____

Day Forty-Five

It blesses Me that you would have the desire to commune with Me even though you are obviously sleepy. Thanks for every effort you made to get up, come before My Presence, sing to Me, and pray in your prayer language. I received every breath it took for you to commune with Me. I applaud the desire of your heart.

There will be times when you will be sleepy and know not what to say, but your spirit will always know exactly what to say. Your spirit lives in the very seat of your heart, My child. Thank you for communing with Me from the bottom of your heart. Know that your day has already been set because you first came to Me, sang praises in worship, allowed the Holy Spirit to pray the perfect prayer. So, go with the flow as I lead and guide you; permit the happenings. I love you, My child. Thanks for your sincere love for Me.

Your Thoughts or Prayer

_____

_____

_____

_____

_____

_____

_____

_____

_____

_____

_____

_____

_____

_____

_____

_____

_____

_____

_____

_____

DAY FORTY-SIX

Need I remind you again to be anxious for nothing? You are concerned, very much concerned about your loved one who's about to decide what you feel will cause long-term regret. Some decisions are costly and irrevocable. You have done well to suggest for your loved one to acknowledge Me and allow Me to direct the path that should be taken.

I have given you insight into the motives of your loved one's heart. It is indeed about escapism. It is a harsh truth that your loved one is trying to avoid. It is an unsafe environment in your loved one's eyes. Your loved one can see the faces of the family members snarling at him. Fear and only fear is what's keeping your loved one from wanting to face those faces in what he perceives as a hostile environment.

Trust Me to direct the decision that your loved one shall make. Trust Me to enable your loved one to face the consequences of the decision that will be made. Whatever happens shall work according to Romans 8:28, for good. This decision is indeed the beginning of a whole new chapter of your loved one facing harsh truths. It is only the

Truth that sets one free. Trust My involvement in the outcome.

Your Thoughts or Prayer

_____

_____

_____

_____

_____

_____

_____

_____

_____

_____

_____

_____

_____

_____

_____

_____

_____

DAY FORTY-SEVEN

You wonder about how effective you are in prayer when you find that you have fallen asleep before Me. The most important thing is that you have made the effort to get out of your bed, to go to your designated prayer area, to lay prostrate before Me, to sing My praises, and to pray in your natural language and in your prayer-language led by the Holy Spirit. What is most important is that you have come to Me. You could have turned over in your bed and chosen not to come. Instead, you did as Jesus did. You came to Me very early in the morning, but while it was still dark (see Mark 1:35). It's the sacrifice that you were willing to make for Me. I will reward you each time you come to Me. Look up the words "come to Me" in the Bible to read the benefits of coming. The Holy Spirit has prayed the perfect prayer through you.

I allowed you to fall asleep because you obviously needed the sleep. I know that you did not get up to come before Me to sleep. Again, you sang praises to Me, prayed, and then you fell asleep. After realizing you had fallen asleep, you immediately started singing praises and praying in the Spirit. With your sacrifices of praise and prayer, I Am most pleased. When you praise and pray, you are not asking for Me to give you anything. Instead, you are praising Me and praying for others. Thank you, My child, for having the heart of an intercessor.

Your Thoughts or Prayer

_____

_____

_____

_____

_____

_____

_____

_____

_____

_____

_____

_____

_____

_____

_____

_____

DAY FORTY-EIGHT

Oh, how I enjoy hearing you sing praises to Me and My Name! You sang "How Excellent Is My Name," and indeed it is. You also sang "Holy, Righteous, and Worthy Is My Name."

Thank you, My child, thank you for singing praises to Me.

You have said thanks to Me for giving you this brand-new day. You have said that you are surrendering yourself to Me and giving this day back to Me so that I may live through you. Thank you, My child. I shall direct your thoughts and open your eyes, ears, and heart for you to be very sensitive and in tune with My Lead and My Voice. How wise and unselfish of you to live your day receptive to My Will for your life today!

Yes, My child, this is how I Am made to feel welcomed in one's life when he/she opens their heart and yields their all to Me. It only allows Me to flourish him/her with more of Me, one day at a time. Thank you for welcoming Me into your God-given day. Act on the idea that I gave you this morning as you prayed. Do it as early as possible. My timing is perfect. I Am moving by My Spirit.

Your Thoughts or Prayer

_____

_____

_____

_____

_____

_____

_____

_____

_____

_____

_____

_____

_____

_____

_____

_____

_____

_____

_____

DAY FORTY-NINE

I delight, My child, to saturate you with My Presence. You have such a love, a delight, and an appetite for Me that I Am delighted to fill your cup to over-flowing this morning. Be all of Me that you can be today, My child. Be sensitive to every sound, movement, and activity. Look for Me and listen for Me all day. I want you to experience this day of walking more closely with Me by practicing My Presence as long as you can hold on to Me today.

I'm bringing Myself to the forefront of your life today. I have found favor with you. Your heart's desire is to be in alignment with Me. Your desire is to look like, talk like, act like, and to be like your Heavenly Father, Daddy. Today, I shall allow you to feel My Presence if you desire, My child. It's up to you to remember that I Am in you and walking right by your side all day. With that in view, purpose to have a victorious day and resort to My Presence as often as you can. I delight to walk with you today, My child. May you feel and enjoy My Presence all day. Thank you for singing your praises to Me. I loved each song. With you, I Am well-pleased. Enjoy yourself in Me today.

Your Thoughts or Prayer

_____

_____

_____

_____

_____

_____

_____

_____

_____

_____

_____

_____

_____

_____

_____

_____

_____

_____

DAY FIFTY

Let not your heart be troubled. Once again, your heart has some unsettling about your relationship with someone. You have done right to share your concerns with Me. Your responsibility is to continue to demonstrate your love. Thank you for sharing your unsettling's with Me. Confession is good for the cleansing of your mind.

Trust Me to vindicate your name, My child. Trust me to put those ones at peace with you. Those who may have malice in their hearts towards you shall become your footstools. Read scriptures concerning footstools. My child, I want you to be at peace in your head and in your heart for them.

Purpose to verbalize love and acceptance for those individuals who are distractors of your peace. You have confessed your faults and thoughts to Me. Replace all questions with loving thoughts for them. Do not let doubt, mistrust, or fear park in your head or heart toward them.

Call their names one by one out loud. Say, "I love _____. I choose to be at peace with _____ in my heart and in my mind."

Your Thoughts or Prayer

_____

_____

_____

_____

_____

_____

_____

_____

_____

_____

_____

_____

_____

_____

_____

_____

_____

_____

_____

_____

_____

_____

_____

DAY FIFTY-ONE

It blesses Me for you and your spouse to desire more of Me. You said that from the crown of your head to the soles of your feet, you want Me to reside, rule, and reign in the inward parts all the way to the marrow of your bones. My child, that's an in-depth, overall desire for which your innermost parts are to be changed. You know that nothing is too difficult or insignificant to Me. Yes, My child, I will do a total makeover of you and your spouse for My Glory. Yes, you have declared your best for Me. How many of My people can truly say that they desire their best for My Glory?

I applaud your desire to give your best and all of yourself to Me for My Glory and not for selfish gain. Thank you for placing your desires at My feet so that I can pour out My Blessings that shall overtake you. Thanks for so unselfishly including your spouse. Only I can change the inward parts and desires of others by changing their mindsets and wills.

Your Thoughts or Prayer

Day Fifty-Two

Thank you, My child, for giving yourself to Me today and for giving your day back to Me. You have given Me a full reign of these twenty-four hours in your day to rule and reign as your Lord. I appreciate your delight in drawing closer to Me. Know that I promise to draw closer to you.

Thank you for ignoring the distraction of phone text beeps that summoned your attention. You got up from your prayer area and came straight to hear from Me. Thank you for putting Me first, for desiring to hear what I would say to you before turning to your phone to hear from others.

Know that I reward you and others who genuinely seek Me with their whole heart. I am so pleased to have you and My faithful few, the remnant, who desire Me more than yourselves. I love you, as you well know. Thank you for receiving My love and for sharing your prayers, words of encourage-ment, and love to others. Know that with you, I Am well-pleased. Enjoy the fullness of My Presence today, My child. Yes, bask in My Presence today. I Am your God, the Ruler of your heart and the universe.

Your Thoughts or Prayer

_____

_____

_____

_____

_____

_____

_____

_____

_____

_____

_____

_____

_____

_____

_____

_____

_____

_____

_____

_____

_____

DAY FIFTY-THREE

You bless Me with your sensitivity to My Spirit. Thank you for singing the song "I Don't Mind Waiting on the Lord." If My people would recognize that I will come, I will come to their rescue for whatever reasons they need Me. I Am their Supplier for everything they need. I do not lack in meeting each of My children's needs. My timing is perfect!

Thank you for reminding others through that song to look to Me and to wait for Me. I Am The Great I Am of infinite promises. Oh, that My people would indeed believe that I Am shall come through for them! If only My people would patiently wait for Me to show up on their behalf. As you have said, My timing is perfect to do whatever needs to be done.

Continue to encourage others to trust Me and to wait patiently for Me. Be anxious for nothing! I shall come, and I shall do. I shall take care of My people. What kind of God would I be if I would not take care of My people? I Am the Faithful God.

Your Thoughts or Prayer

_____

_____

_____

_____

_____

_____

_____

_____

_____

_____

_____

_____

_____

_____

_____

_____

_____

_____

Day Fifty-Four

What a delight you have been to Me this morning! How unselfish were your prayers to Me! You said, "Father, I desire to take nothing from You. I just want to give You all of me." That blesses Me, My child. I receive all that you have to give of yourself, and I will give you more of me. How's that? What an exchange! Do you recall the song "You Can't Beat God's Giving"? Well, it's true, My child.

What can one give to Me in the invisible realm? I receive your love, your heart, your desires, your concerns, your hopes, your dreams, your inspirations, your aspirations, your intentions, and your plans. I receive your thinking about the right thing and the wrong thing. I receive your longings, the right ones and the wrong ones. Enjoy more of Me. It's the exchange that we share. Thank you for giving yourself to Me.

Your Thoughts or Prayer

_____

_____

_____

_____

_____

_____

_____

_____

_____

_____

_____

_____

_____

_____

_____

_____

_____

_____

_____

_____

Day Fifty-Five

With you, I Am well pleased. You desire to have more of Me. I shall give you as much as you desire. The secret to getting more of Me is to the emptying of yourself in order to make room for more of Me.

Many are satisfied with getting Me, and they will gladly shout, "As long as I've got Jesus, I don't need anything and nobody else." That is not truth. See, the more that they have of Me, the more they realize the need to share Me with others. I gave everyone Me. What are you and others to do with Me? You are to give Me to others.

Many are willing to give money, stuff, things, and accolades of praise. I Am the Gift of gifts. What is the Best Gift that one can give to another? It is an awareness of Me. I Am the Best Gift ever.

Many have received Me, but they don't recognize Me as a gift. Therefore, they have not fully embraced Me. If one receives a pretty necklace or a pretty piece of clothing, they will wear it and show it to others. Many have received Me but have tucked Me away. But those who are My remnant, true followers, are so very unselfishly sharing Me with as many people as they can.

If a person receives a gift but does not realize the full value of it, they will either abuse it or neglect it. They will misuse or mishandle it. Far too many of My people are neglecting Me. What is the purpose of receiving a gift if it is not being valued?

Furthermore, many misuse Me by viewing Me as a genie. They are constantly asking, "Father, will You do this or Father, will You do that? Father will You heal me; give me; forgive me; protect me?" If I fail to do whatever is asked, they then say in their hearts, "I don't really need God because He's not doing what I asked Him to do, or it's taking Him too long to come through for me." Far too many are more excited about what I can do for them rather than Who I Am. I Am all they need. If ever they will take the time to get to know Me, only then can they imitate Me or present Me to others.

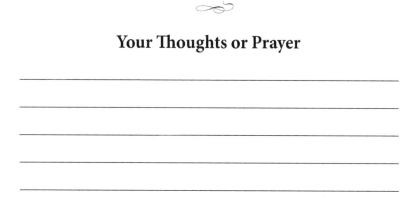

Your Thoughts or Prayer

_____

_____

_____

_____

_____

DAY FIFTY-SIX

This morning, your prayers are on target; you covered all the bases. You have a very clear understanding of "Who I Am" and who you are in Me. The longing of My heart is that My people would desire to get to know me, Who I Truly Am, and who I truly want them to become in Me. Only then can they receive, walk in, and live in the fullness of life. What is life without the knowledge of Who I Am? The answer is "emptiness."

My people are walking around in empty shells. They lack My Presence. They won't be able to recognize Me because they do not know Who I Am. The only way that they can get to know Me is to spend time each day reading My Word and praying. That's when I will reveal Myself to him and her.

There is no greater joy than I will have but for My people to get to know Me. Then, they will want to spend more time with Me. I will constantly reward them with My Love, Joy, Peace, and all the rest of the Fruit of the Spirit. Such is the abundance of life.

Your Thoughts or Prayer

_____

_____

_____

_____

_____

_____

_____

_____

_____

_____

_____

_____

_____

_____

_____

_____

_____

_____

_____

_____

_____

_____

_____

Day Fifty-Seven

It blesses Me to hear you say that you desire Truth in the inward parts. My Truth desired is My Truth delivered. My Truth delivered is My Truth saturated. My Truth saturated is My Truth permeated into the very core of your being. It is indeed My Truth that shall set you free from yourself and from everything that would hinder you from being all I have purposed you to be, free from the deception of the enemy.

Far too many of My people are walking around with emptiness. Even though they speak My Word, they fail to embrace My Word and allow it to saturate their hearts. They have My Word in their mind and on their tongues, but they have not let My Words penetrate their hearts, the very core of their being. My Word is truth, and truth on the inside will eradicate spiritual pollution. Truth on the inside will build up what has been torn down in the hearts of My people.

A pure heart is what I seek. My Word is the only thing that will purify the heart. Humility will come when My people saturate their hearts with My Word. Then, I will cleanse them from all the spiritual heart disease that is caused by the lack of My Word.

Your Thoughts or Prayer

_____

_____

_____

_____

_____

_____

_____

_____

_____

_____

_____

_____

_____

_____

_____

_____

_____

_____

DAY FIFTY-EIGHT

I do recognize where you are, and I applaud you. You are correct: you do have the victory over depression, doubt, fear, sickness, disease, and unbelief. I Am the Victory who lives inside of you. The closer you draw nearer to Me, the closer I draw near to you. Therefore, the more your faith, your belief, and your boldness come to you, the more of My Power is manifested to you, and the more victories we shall have.

You are right to ask of Me to give you a heart of compassion, not a pity party, but compassion for those who are captivated by fear, doubt, depression, and the likes. And as you draw nearer to Me, you shall take on more of Me and My Compassion.

You are correct, My child, it is a faith walk. Many and far too many of My people say with their heads and with their mouths, "I believe," and they are hopeful of believing. But great faith says, "It is so," and indeed, it is so. My Word is Sovereign over all. My Word shall not come back void. My Word has been spoken, done, and finished. And according to your faith, be it unto you. You are indeed the partaker of My Word, and by faith, it shall be granted to you. You shall have it, and you shall do it. Yes, indeed, you have the victory. Ask, and it shall be granted.

Your Thoughts or Prayer

_____

_____

_____

_____

_____

_____

_____

_____

_____

_____

_____

_____

_____

_____

_____

_____

_____

Day Fifty-Nine

You are indeed excited about Me. The energy bunny has nothing on you. You are going to fight and do great exploits for Me. Has not this been the daily cry of your heart for a long time? You might not have asked me specifically for a while, and you might have forgotten that you have ever asked. Not only have you asked it for yourself, but you have asked it for your young grandsons. Have I not promised to give you the desires of your heart?

It blesses Me, My child, that you have often expressed not wanting to ask Me for natural things because you do not want to prevent yourself from receiving better things I may have in store. You have said that you shall ask Me, though, for spiritual things. You are so on point, My child. That which is on the invisible realm is eternal where moth, dust, and rust shall never take place. The cankerworm cannot eat a hole or destroy anything in the invisible realm.

Continue to set your eyes on the heavenly realm, that which you cannot see in the natural. Set your eyes on things above, and expect to receive from Me. I shall reveal more of the unseen to you because you have set your heart and mind to look up and live in Me. I give you Me and the fullness thereof. Freely receive it, My yielded one.

Your Thoughts or Prayer

_____

_____

_____

_____

_____

_____

_____

_____

_____

_____

_____

_____

_____

_____

_____

_____

_____

DAY SIXTY

It has been time well spent with you this morning. Oh, how I have enjoyed your visitation and the concerns of your heart. Thank you for yielding to Me. Thank you for being concerned about everything that concerns Me, as you know that I Am likewise concerned about everything that concerns you. With you, My child, I Am well-pleased.

My dear, know that if you purpose to draw closer to Me by reading My Word, praying to Me, and spending time in My Presence, you shall have more and more of Me. I give you all of Me as you give Me all of you. Oh, the beauty of the exchange between you and Me, and the fullness thereof.

Continue to set your sight and your affections on Me and the things above. I have already opened the heavens for you. Take hold of Me, and know that you shall surely receive the fullness of Me. You have found the secret of living the abundant life on earth. It is in seeking Me. As you continue to seek Me and My heart, I shall reward you. Continue to live in Me and watch Me perform.

Your Thoughts or Prayer

_____

_____

_____

_____

_____

_____

_____

_____

_____

_____

_____

_____

_____

_____

_____

_____

_____

_____

_____

_____

_____

Day _____ cont'd

_____

_____

_____

_____

_____

_____

_____

_____

_____

_____

_____

_____

_____

_____

_____

_____

_____

_____

_____

_____

_____

_____

_____

_____

DAY _____ CONT'D

DAY _____ CONT'D

DAY _____ CONT'D

DAY _____ CONT'D

Day _____ cont'd

DAY _____ CONT'D

_____

_____

_____

_____

_____

_____

_____

_____

_____

_____

_____

_____

_____

_____

_____

_____

_____

_____

_____

_____

_____

_____

_____

D<small>AY</small> _____ <small>CONT'D</small>

DAY _____ CONT'D

DAY _____ CONT'D

Day _____ cont'd

DAY _____ CONT'D

DAY _____ CONT'D

_____

_____

_____

_____

_____

_____

_____

_____

_____

_____

_____

_____

_____

_____

_____

_____

_____

_____

_____

_____

_____

_____

DAY _____ CONT'D

DAY _____ CONT'D

.